P9-BYJ-887

United States Presidents

Franklin D. Roosevelt

Paul Joseph
ABDO Publishing Company

visit us at
www.abdopub.com

Published by ABDO Publishing Company 4940 Viking Drive, Edina, Minnesota 55435.
Copyright © 2000 by Abdo Consulting Group, Inc. International copyrights reserved in
all countries. No part of this book may be reproduced in any form without written
permission from the publisher.

Printed in the United States.

Interior Photo credits: AP/Wide World, SuperStock, Archive, Corbis-Bettmann

Contributing editors: Robert Italia, Tamara L. Britton, K.M. Brielmaier, Kate A. Furlong

Library of Congress Cataloging-in-Publication Data

Joseph, Paul, 1970-
    Franklin D. Roosevelt / Paul Joseph
        p. cm. -- (United States presidents)
    Includes index.
    Summary: A biography of the only man to be elected president of the United
States four times.
    ISBN 1-56239-813-X
    1. Roosevelt, Franklin D. (Franklin Delano), 1882-1945--Juvenile literature. 2.
Presidents--United States--Biography--Juvenile literature. [1. Roosevelt,
Franklin D. (Franklin Delano), 1882-1945. 2. Presidents.] I. Title. II. Series:
United States presidents (Edina, Minn.)
E807.J647   1999
973.917'092--dc21
    [B]   97-50199
                                                              CIP
                                                               AC

Contents

Franklin D. Roosevelt

*F*ranklin Delano Roosevelt was elected president four times. No other U.S. president has been elected more than twice. President Roosevelt led the country through two of the worst problems in the twentieth century.

Roosevelt became president in 1933 during the **Great Depression**. Millions of Americans were out of work. Roosevelt's plans created jobs and helped the economy. Some of his plans were questioned at the time. But today, many are still used.

President Roosevelt was one of the great leaders during **World War II**. His leadership helped end the war.

Roosevelt also had personal challenges. Few Americans knew that he could not walk without help. When he was 39 years old, Roosevelt contracted **polio**. This disease **paralyzed** his legs. Despite his paralysis, Roosevelt became one of the most important presidents in American history.

Franklin D. Roosevelt

Franklin D. Roosevelt (1882-1945)
Thirty-second President

BORN: January 30, 1882

PLACE OF BIRTH: Hyde Park, New York

ANCESTRY: Dutch, Huguenot, English, Swedish, Finnish

FATHER: James Roosevelt (1828-1900)

MOTHER: Sara Delano Roosevelt (1854-1941)

WIFE: Anna Eleanor Roosevelt (1884-1962)

CHILDREN: Six: 5 boys, 1 girl

EDUCATION: Private tutors, Groton School, Harvard University, Columbia University

RELIGION: Episcopalian

OCCUPATION: Lawyer

MILITARY SERVICE: None

POLITICAL PARTY: Democrat

OFFICES HELD: Member of the New York state senate, assistant
secretary of the navy, governor of New York

AGE AT INAUGURATION: 51

YEARS SERVED: 1933-1937, 1937-1941, 1941-1945,
1945-died in office

VICE PRESIDENTS: John Garner (1933-1937) (1937-1941), Henry
Wallace (1941-1945), and Harry S. Truman (1945)

DIED: April 12, 1945, Warm Springs, Georgia, age 63

CAUSE OF DEATH: Stroke

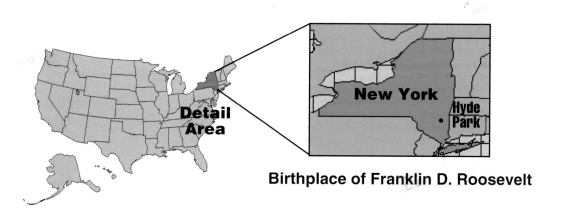

Birthplace of Franklin D. Roosevelt

Young Franklin

*F*ranklin Delano Roosevelt was born near Hyde Park, New York, on January 30, 1882. He was the only child of James and Sara Roosevelt.

James was a wealthy landowner and a railroad **executive**. And he was a **diplomat** under President Grover Cleveland. Sara came from a wealthy shipping family.

The Roosevelts lived in a large home along the Hudson River. They had servants and maids. Franklin was educated at home by tutors. The family took vacations at their summer home on Campobello Island near Eastport, Maine.

Franklin's parents had strict rules. He rarely got into trouble. And he was a good student.

Franklin had many hobbies. When he was 10, he took an interest in birds. He often went into the woods to watch and listen to them. Franklin also liked sailing and stamp collecting.

When he was 14, Franklin entered Groton School in Massachusetts. Groton was a boarding school for young men.

Franklin earned average grades at Groton. He was small and not very athletic. But he was active in sports. Franklin was on the football team practice squad. And he was the student manager of the baseball team.

Franklin with his mother, Sara

Law School and Eleanor

*A*fter graduation, Roosevelt went to Harvard University in Cambridge, Massachusetts. He studied history, economics, and science. In his last year of college, Roosevelt became the president and editor of the school newspaper, the *Crimson*.

Roosevelt graduated from Harvard in 1904. Then he attended Columbia University Law School in New York City. Roosevelt married Anna Eleanor Roosevelt on March 17, 1905. Anna, who went by Eleanor, was Roosevelt's sixth cousin. President Theodore Roosevelt was Eleanor's uncle. He attended the wedding.

Franklin and Eleanor had six children. Anna Eleanor was born in 1906. James was born in 1907, and Elliott in 1910. Franklin, Jr., was born in 1914, and John in 1916. Another boy was born in 1909. He died while still a baby.

In 1907, Roosevelt began working as a lawyer for a large New York City law firm. But he found the job boring. He began thinking about working in politics.

Democratic party leaders believed Roosevelt could be successful in New York politics. The Roosevelt name was well-known. And he had the wealth to run a strong campaign. They asked him to run for state senator in 1910.

Roosevelt jumped at the chance. He had learned from Theodore Roosevelt that political work was exciting.

Roosevelt toured the state by car. He made many speeches. Voters liked what they heard and elected him to the senate.

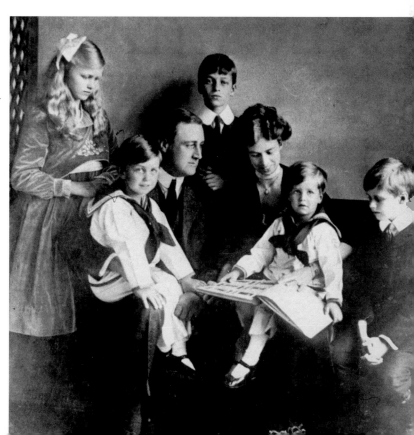

Franklin and Eleanor with their five children in 1919: (left to right) Anna, Franklin Jr., James, John, and Elliott

On to Washington

*S*tate senator Roosevelt introduced bills to protect public lands, forests, and parks. He introduced a bill that loaned money to farmers. And he supported a bill to lower working hours for boys aged 16 to 21. Roosevelt was re-elected in 1912.

That year, Roosevelt worked for Woodrow Wilson's presidential campaign. He made speeches and wrote letters. He also led 150 **delegates** who supported Wilson at the **Democratic National Convention**. Wilson won the election.

Roosevelt's work impressed President Wilson and Democratic party leaders. Wilson named Roosevelt assistant secretary of the navy in 1913.

In 1914, Roosevelt ran for the U.S. Senate. But party leaders felt he was too inexperienced. Roosevelt did not win the election.

Roosevelt remained assistant secretary of the navy. He made sure the navy was ready for any type of war. He kept the ships in good condition. And he looked for ways to improve them. He also worked well with admirals, department employees, and party leaders.

America entered **World War I** in 1917. Roosevelt openly supported the war against Germany. And he worked hard to make the navy bigger and stronger.

In 1918, he visited the front lines in Europe. By now, Roosevelt had gained valuable experience, political contacts, and national exposure. He was ready to run for a higher political office.

Europe during World War I

Roosevelt's Challenge

*I*n 1920, **Democrats** chose Governor James Cox of Ohio as their presidential candidate. They chose Roosevelt to run for vice president.

Roosevelt ran a strong campaign. He traveled the country by train. He made more than 1,000 speeches. Cox and Roosevelt lost the election. But Roosevelt gained national attention.

Roosevelt returned to New York City. There, he formed a law firm. In August 1921, Roosevelt became sick while on vacation at Campobello. He had a high fever. And he could not move his legs. About a month later, Roosevelt learned he had **polio**. He would never walk without help again.

Roosevelt's political career seemed to be over. Most people thought that a man in a wheelchair could never be elected to political office.

With Eleanor's help, Roosevelt fought the disease. In 1924, he went to a resort in Warm Springs, Georgia. There, he treated his **paralysis** in the resort's hot spring water.

Roosevelt decided to help others who suffered from **polio**. In 1927, he bought the resort. Then he formed the Georgia Warm Springs Foundation for the study and treatment of polio.

Roosevelt hired a doctor and a **physical therapist** to take care of patients. Polio victims from all over the country went to Warm Springs. They received treatment and swam in warm mineral water. Roosevelt spent several months each year at Warm Springs.

Roosevelt also kept active in politics. He wrote many letters to party leaders. He often met with them in Washington, D.C., on his way to and from Warm Springs.

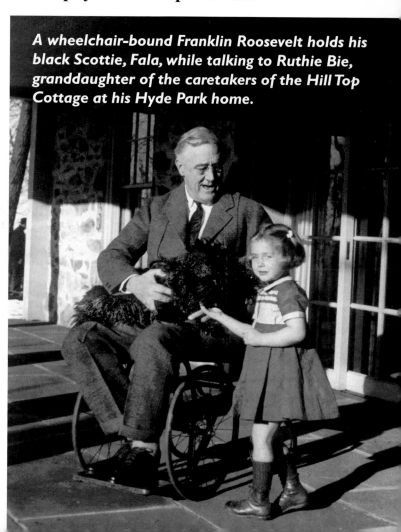

A wheelchair-bound Franklin Roosevelt holds his black Scottie, Fala, while talking to Ruthie Bie, granddaughter of the caretakers of the Hill Top Cottage at his Hyde Park home.

The Making of the Thirty-second United States President

1882
Born
January 30
in Hyde
Park, New
York

1896
Enters
Groton
School

1900
Enters
Harvard
University

1910
Elected
state senator
in New York

1913
Appointed
assistant
secretary of the
navy

1921
Contracts polio
virus

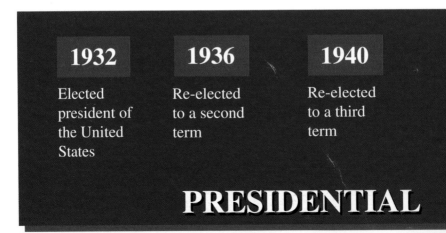

1932
Elected
president of
the United
States

1936
Re-elected
to a second
term

1940
Re-elected
to a third
term

PRESIDENTIAL

Franklin D. Roosevelt

"The only thing we have to fear is fear itself."

1904
Enters
Columbia
University
Law School

1905
Marries
Anna
Eleanor
Roosevelt

1907
Works as
a lawyer
in New
York City

Historic Events
during Roosevelt's Presidency

★ Walt Disney releases the movie *Bambi*

★ Amelia Earhart first woman to
fly solo across the Atlantic Ocean

★ Frances Perkins becomes first
female presidential cabinet member

1927
Establishes the
Georgia
Warm Springs
Foundation

1928
Elected
governor
of New
York

1930
Re-elected
governor of
New York

1941
U.S. declares
war on Japan

1944
Re-elected
to a fourth
term

1945
Yalta conference
with Churchill
and Stalin;
Roosevelt dies
on April 12

YEARS

Governor Roosevelt

*I*n 1928, the **Democratic** party asked Roosevelt to run for governor of New York. Roosevelt won the election easily.

Governor Roosevelt passed laws that reduced working hours. He passed laws that lowered the cost of electricity. And he passed laws to help farmers. In 1930, Roosevelt was re-elected. It was the biggest election victory in state history.

By 1931, the **Great Depression** was at its worst. Many New Yorkers were out of work. Governor Roosevelt formed a work program for New Yorkers who needed jobs.

In 1932, the Democratic party chose Roosevelt to run for president. Roosevelt flew to the **Democratic National Convention** in Chicago, Illinois, to address the party. "I pledge you," he said, "I pledge myself, to a new deal for the American people."

Roosevelt traveled the country and gave speeches. He promised national programs to help farmers, small banks, and home owners.

Americans were weary of the Great Depression. Roosevelt's New Deal seemed to be the answer.

Governor Roosevelt

President Roosevelt

*I*n November 1932, Roosevelt defeated President Herbert Hoover in the election. On March 4, 1933, Roosevelt was **inaugurated** at the Capitol in Washington, D.C. He told the country that "the only thing we have to fear is fear itself." Roosevelt's speech gave Americans hope.

In Roosevelt's first 100 days, he signed many of his programs into law. He called these programs the National Recovery Act (NRA).

The Civilian Conservation Corps (CCC) was started in 1933. It preserved the nation's natural resources. It also gave jobs to men aged 18 to 25. The men planted trees, and dug **reservoirs** and ditches. They built dams, bridges, and fire towers. And they cleared beaches and built campgrounds.

The Agriculture Adjustment Act (AAA) also was created in 1933. It limited the amount of crops farmers could grow. This kept crop prices from falling, which helped farmers make money.

Roosevelt created the Works Progress Administration (WPA) in 1935. The WPA created jobs for millions of people. They built public buildings, bridges, dams, and houses.

President Roosevelt also signed into law the Social Security Act. This gave money to people who could not find jobs, or were too old to work. It also gave money to people who could not pay for medical care. And it gave money to people who needed help to support their children.

President Roosevelt explained his New Deal plans over the radio. These broadcasts were called "fireside chats." He gave them from the White House. Americans felt that Roosevelt was in their living rooms, by the fireside, talking to them personally.

Some people called Roosevelt's programs unconstitutional. They claimed Roosevelt was abusing his power.

In 1936, Roosevelt was up for re-election. During his campaign, he said, "I am the issue. You are either for me or against me." Roosevelt won the biggest election victory in U.S. history.

Roosevelt delivers a "fireside chat" to Americans.

The Seven "Hats" of the U.S. President

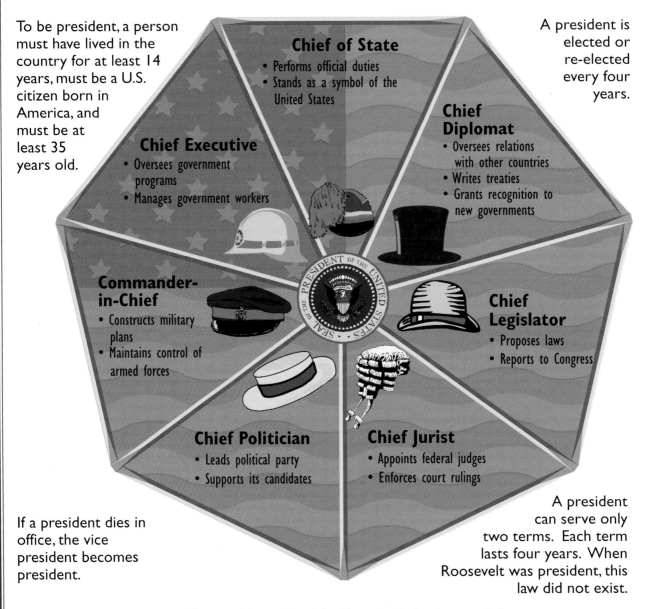

To be president, a person must have lived in the country for at least 14 years, must be a U.S. citizen born in America, and must be at least 35 years old.

A president is elected or re-elected every four years.

Chief of State
- Performs official duties
- Stands as a symbol of the United States

Chief Diplomat
- Oversees relations with other countries
- Writes treaties
- Grants recognition to new governments

Chief Executive
- Oversees government programs
- Manages government workers

Commander-in-Chief
- Constructs military plans
- Maintains control of armed forces

Chief Legislator
- Proposes laws
- Reports to Congress

Chief Politician
- Leads political party
- Supports its candidates

Chief Jurist
- Appoints federal judges
- Enforces court rulings

If a president dies in office, the vice president becomes president.

A president can serve only two terms. Each term lasts four years. When Roosevelt was president, this law did not exist.

As president, Franklin Roosevelt had seven jobs.

The Three Branches of the U.S. Government

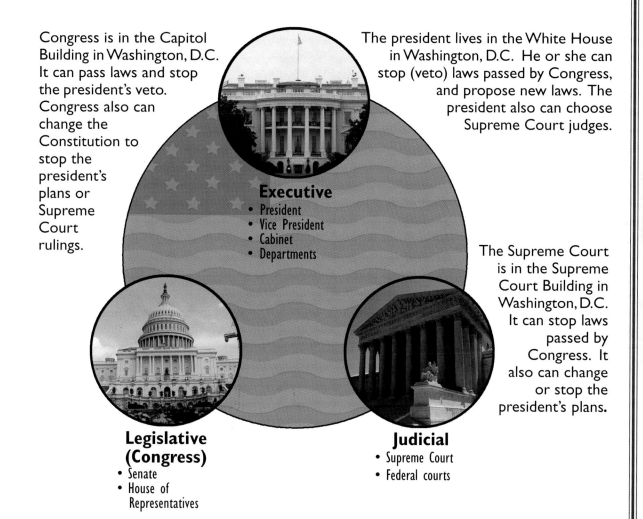

Congress is in the Capitol Building in Washington, D.C. It can pass laws and stop the president's veto. Congress also can change the Constitution to stop the president's plans or Supreme Court rulings.

The president lives in the White House in Washington, D.C. He or she can stop (veto) laws passed by Congress, and propose new laws. The president also can choose Supreme Court judges.

Executive
- President
- Vice President
- Cabinet
- Departments

The Supreme Court is in the Supreme Court Building in Washington, D.C. It can stop laws passed by Congress. It also can change or stop the president's plans.

Legislative (Congress)
- Senate
- House of Representatives

Judicial
- Supreme Court
- Federal courts

The U.S. Constitution formed three government branches. Each branch has power over the others. So, no single group or person can control the country. The Constitution calls this "separation of powers."

World War II

*I*n 1940, President Roosevelt thought about retiring to Hyde Park. He had served two terms. No president in U.S. history had served more. But Roosevelt felt a sense of duty to continue as president.

World War II had begun in Europe. Germany had seized much of Europe, including France. Now, Germany was threatening Great Britain.

The British fought hard. But they were running out of supplies. Roosevelt knew the British would need help to survive. But most Americans did not want to join the war.

While dealing with the problems in Europe, Roosevelt decided to run for a third term. Forty-nine million people voted in the election. It was the largest voter turnout in U.S. history. President Roosevelt won a third term.

After the election, Roosevelt arranged the Lend-Lease Act. The United States would lend ships and supplies to its **allies** fighting Germany. Now, the United States could help Great Britain without joining the war.

EUROPE DURING WORLD WAR II (1939-1945)

Detail Area

Atlantic Ocean

Finland

Norway

Sweden

Estonia

Latvia

Baltic Sea

Lithuania

Soviet Union

Northern Ireland

Denmark

Ireland

Netherlands

Great Britain

East Prussia

Poland

Germany

Belgium

Switzerland

Liechtenstein

Slovakia

France

Hungary

Romania

Yugoslavia

Black Sea

Portugal

Adriatic Sea

Italy

Bulgaria

Spain

Turkey

Albania

Greece

Aegean Sea

Mediterranean Sea

AFRICA

On December 7, 1941, Japanese planes staged a surprise attack on the U.S. naval base at Pearl Harbor, Hawaii. The Japanese sunk ships, bombed airfields and buildings, and killed more than 2,000 Americans.

The next day, Roosevelt asked Congress for a declaration of war on Japan. In his famous speech, he called December 7 "a date which will live in infamy." By December 11, the U.S. was at war with the other **Axis Powers** of Germany and Italy.

Roosevelt made many trips to Europe. He helped keep the **Allies**—America, Great Britain, France, and the Soviet Union—united in the war against the Axis Powers.

Another presidential election occurred in 1944. The United States was still fighting the war. But the Axis Powers had suffered major defeats.

Roosevelt was in poor health. But he believed that he should remain president. He won a fourth term. It was his smallest election victory.

Opposite page:
The USS Arizona is in flames after the Japanese attack on Pearl Harbor.

In February 1945, Roosevelt went to a conference in Yalta, Ukraine, in the Soviet Union. There, he met with **Allied** leaders. The war in Europe was almost over. They discussed the end of the war, and Europe's future.

Roosevelt returned to America. He took a long vacation at Warm Springs. Around 1:00 P.M. on April 12, 1945, Roosevelt rubbed his forehead and said, "I have a terrific pain in the back of my head." Then he collapsed. Less than three hours later, he died of a stroke.

Roosevelt's death shocked the nation. He had been the country's leader for more than a decade. Roosevelt was buried at his home in Hyde Park. **World War II** ended in September 1945.

Franklin D. Roosevelt was one of America's most important presidents. He led the country for twelve years. He helped end the **Great Depression** with his government programs. He established social security. And he helped bring an end to World War II.

British prime minister Winston Churchill (left), Franklin Roosevelt, and Soviet Union premier Joseph Stalin meet in Yalta.

Fun Facts

- Franklin Roosevelt was such a popular president that the White House staff measured his mail by the pound.

- In 1939, Roosevelt became the first president to appear on television. Few people had televisions at the time. Most TVs had six-inch screens.

- President Roosevelt was the first president to fly in an airplane while in office.

- American women were given the right to vote in 1920. President Roosevelt's mother, Sara, was the first woman able to vote for her son in a presidential election.

- Roosevelt collected nearly 25,000 stamps in his lifetime. At his death, his collection was worth millions of dollars.

Glossary

allies - countries that agree to help each other in times of need. During World War II, Great Britain, France, the United States, and the Soviet Union were called the Allies.

Axis Powers - Germany, Italy, and Japan during World War II.

delegate - a person who represents voters.

Democrat - one of the two main political parties in the United States. Democrats are often more liberal and believe in more government.

Democratic National Convention - a national meeting held every four years by the Democratic party to choose a presidential candidate.

diplomat - a person who deals with representatives of other countries.

executive - a person in a high position in a company.

Great Depression - the failure of the U.S. economy starting in 1929 and lasting through the 1930s. A depression is a time when business is slow, and people are out of work.

inaugurate - when a person is sworn into a political office.

paralysis - a lessening or loss of the power of motion or feeling in any part of the body.

physical therapist - a person who helps injured or ill people regain the use of their muscles.

polio - (poliomyelitis) a disease that sometimes causes a paralysis of the legs.

reservoir - a place where something is stored.

World War I - 1914 to 1918, fought in Europe. The United States, Great Britian, France, Russia, and their allies were on one side. Germany, Austria-Hungary, and their allies were on the other side. The war began when Archduke Ferdinand of Austria was assassinated. America joined the war in 1917 because Germany began attacking ships that weren't involved in the war.

World War II - 1939 to 1945, fought in Europe, Asia, and Africa. The United States, France, Great Britain, the Soviet Union, and their allies were on one side. Germany, Italy, Japan, and their allies were on the other side. The war began when Germany invaded Poland. America entered the war in 1941 after Japan bombed Pearl Harbor, Hawaii.

Internet Sites

United States Presidents Information Page
http://historyoftheworld.com/soquel/prez.htm
Links to information about United States presidents. This site is very informative, with biographies on every president as well as speeches and debates, and other links.

The Presidents of the United States of America
http://www.whitehouse.gov/WH/glimpse/presidents/html/presidents.html
This site is from the White House. With an introduction from President Bill Clinton and biographies that include each president's inaugural address, this site is excellent. Get information on White House history, art in the White House, first ladies, first families, and much more.

POTUS—Presidents of the United States
http://www.ipl.org/ref/POTUS/
In this resource you will find background information, election results, cabinet members, presidency highlights, and some odd facts on each of the presidents. Links to biographies, historical documents, audio and video files, and other presidential sites are also included to enrich this site.

These sites are subject to change. Go to your favorite search engine and type in United States presidents for more sites.

Pass It On

History enthusiasts: educate readers around the country by passing on information you've learned about presidents or other important people who have changed history. Share your little-known facts and interesting stories. We want to hear from you!

To get posted on the ABDO Publishing Company Web site, email us at:
history@abdopub.com
Visit the ABDO Publishing Company Web site at www.abdopub.com

Index

A
Agriculture Adjustment Act (AAA) 20
assistant secretary of the navy 12

B
birth 8

C
children 10
Civilian Conservation Corps (CCC) 20
Cleveland, President Grover 8
Columbia University 10
Cox, James 14

D
death 28
Democratic party 11, 12, 18

E
education 8, 9, 10

F
fireside chats 21

G
Georgia Warm Springs Foundation 15
governor of New York 18
Great Depression 4, 18, 28
Groton School 8, 9

H
Harvard *Crimson* 10
Harvard University 10
hobbies 8, 9
Hoover, President Herbert 20

L
lawyer 10, 14
Lend-Lease Act 24

N
National Recovery Act (NRA) 20
Navy, U.S. 12, 13
New Deal 18, 21

P
Pearl Harbor 26
polio 4, 14, 15
president 18-28
presidential elections 18, 21, 24, 26

R
Roosevelt, Anna Eleanor (wife) 10, 14
Roosevelt, James (father) 8
Roosevelt, President Theodore (cousin) 10, 11
Roosevelt, Sara Delano (mother) 8

S
senate, New York 11
Senate, U.S. 12
senator, state 12
Social Security Act 21, 28

V
vice presidential campaign 14

W
Wilson, President Woodrow 12
Works Progress Administration (WPA) 20
World War I 13
World War II 4, 24, 28

Y
Yalta 28